A Gift of Growth

For

. . . .

From

. . . .

Enabling

Enabling

by

by

JUDITH M. KNOWLTON
and
REBECCA D. CHAITIN

Hazelden
Publishing

Hazelden Publishing
Center City, Minnesota 55012
hazelden.org/bookstore

©1985 by Judith M. Knowlton
and Rebecca D. Chaitin
All rights reserved
Published 1985
Printed in the United States of America

ISBN: 978-1-59285-746-3

Cover design by Madeline Berglund
Interior design and typesetting by Madeline Berglund

Contents

This is a companion book to *Detachment: Seven Simple Steps,* which ought to be read first.

Enabling

. . . .

Living with alcoholism is lousy living at best. By now you have probably put immense amounts of time, energy, and effort into making it tolerable. But the painful truth is, *it hasn't worked.* And deep down, you know it!

When, at long last, you swallow your pride and "go public" by seeking help in Al-Anon or private counseling, almost immediately you get a shock. You are told that everything you've been doing has been "enabling" the alcoholic to *stay sick!*

The word itself is confusing. Surely "enabling" means to help someone? Not when dealing with alcoholism! In this context, enabling means *helping to preserve, protect, and maintain the addiction.*

Have you really been doing all that? And if so, how could you have failed to recognize it? It's simple. Enabling happens when you behave as you were brought up to do—when you put up a brave front, when you work to keep a peaceful and stable home, when you try to protect everyone around you from pain and suffering—in short, *when you are doing the very best you can!*

How do you stop enabling? Simply by *rethinking everything you've ever learned to do!*

Keep in mind that the alcoholic only does or says as much as he★ needs to in order to protect his drinking—his *addiction*. Once alcoholism takes hold, that's his first and only priority. As you look at your own behavior, quietly begin to observe what he does to maneuver you into *helping* him maintain his drinking.

Unfortunately, in our society it seems that everything conspires to help an alcoholic drink, especially in the early years when his consumption is probably excessive but seems sufficiently "controlled" to be socially acceptable. Later on, when the drinking becomes more unpredictable—sometimes relatively normal, sometimes totally uncontrolled—you keep hoping it's just a passing phase, that it will get better. Or you believe the alcoholic's (sincere) morning-after promise that "This time it's going to be different." The descent into alcoholism can be so gradual that everyone is lulled into false hope—including the alcoholic.

But the fact is, *alcoholism is a progressive disease that only*

★"He" can just as easily be "she."

gets worse, never better. The earlier you and others around the alcoholic learn to stop enabling, the greater the likelihood that he will come to recognize his condition and begin his recovery—before brain damage and long-term addiction make such recognition difficult or even impossible.

Co-alcoholics (a short-cut term for those affected by an alcoholic) are motivated to enable for various compelling social and personal reasons. These reasons often appear to be good and even generous—but in the presence of alcoholism they become twisted and misused. Let's examine some of them to see how they actually perpetuate the addiction.

Peace at Any Price

. . . .

Trying to keep a calm home or a balanced relationship is a full-time job. It takes effort and dedication. But when alcoholism enters the picture, the pendulum of daily living swings wildly between the extremes of hyperkinetic craziness and dull, drained exhaustion. Yet every action you take to bring things back to a stable middle ground will force you into a position *contrary* to your own best interests.

If this seems paradoxical, ask yourself these questions:

- Do you find yourself shushing the children when the alcoholic makes unreasonable demands, rather than supporting the children's *reasonable* position?

- Does the threat of the alcoholic's anger send you running to do his bidding even if what he's demanding is *wrong?*

- Have you become ever more skillful at taking on extra tasks (dropping the good things you'd *really* like to be doing) just to placate him or to avoid verbal or physical abuse?

In other words, *have you betrayed your own standards and accepted the unacceptable as a trade-off for "a little peace and quiet"?*

This kind of "peace" has a high price indeed. The constant tension damages you in many subtle ways. It keeps you from paying attention to your own life, pleasures, and needs. Over a long period of time, it may result in subtle inner erosion and physical symptoms. Maybe that's the price you've unwittingly been paying. We doubt if you recognized the connection.

In children, the effects emerge as hostility, withdrawal, poor sleep or school habits, frenetic overachieving, outright anger and violence, or even ulcers. Some peace!

Enabling has yet another consequence: the alcoholic is behaving irresponsibly and unacceptably. His addiction leads him to make childishly self-centered, irrational demands—and everyone dances to his tune! To him, it seems that things are working out just fine. In fact, the more he drinks and the more unreasonable he becomes, the more effort you put into doing it *his* way. Isn't that insane? You bet it is! The actual price of "peace at any price" is accelerated drinking and all the horrors that go with it.

The Conspiracy of Silence

. . . .

If you are like most of us, you were taught not to wash your dirty linen in public. You were expected to protect the family image and endorse a "what will the neighbors think?" mentality. To some extent, consideration of others' opinions is necessary in any organized society, but it can be carried much too far.

Alcoholic behavior is hurtful, crude, intimidating, violent—and acutely embarrassing. But if you say and do nothing, you allow the alcoholic to remain blissfully unaware of the effect his actions have on you. In fact, *your silence tells him that his behavior is okay!* Unless he is told that something is wrong, it is human and natural for him to assume that what he is doing is perfectly acceptable.

The need to avoid embarrassment is a potent motivator. Most of us will go to great lengths to avoid being embarrassed or embarrassing someone else. But if you allow this need to direct just one of your actions, you're on the road to full-blown enabling!

7

It's true that if you speak up, you'll find yourself standing uncomfortably at center stage. Does this fear keep you silent? Consider the consequences. Say you're at a party and the alcoholic has gotten drunk (what else!). You don't want to call attention to yourself by pointing out the obvious, so you slink silently into the passenger seat of the car for the drive home.

What message have you given? You have told the alcoholic: first, that he is not drunk enough to be out of control, and second, that you trust his drunk driving enough to put your *life* in his hands. *Your motive is clear enough*—"I'd rather be dead than embarrassed"—plus you've allowed *him* to maintain the comfortable delusion that he's in control of himself. Think about it. *That's crazy!*

You must never make the mistake of assuming that he really *knows* how you feel about his drinking. No way! In this world, there are no mind-readers. If you haven't spoken up, he *doesn't* know! He's in a sedated state anyway (from the sedative drug alcohol), and *your silence means consent*.

The conspiracy of silence surrounding alcoholism is pervasive. It affects neighbors and friends, doctors and counselors, but especially those within the immediate family group. In fact, others may be taking their cue from *you*. If you act as if "everything-is-fine-thank-you-just-fine," how is anyone else supposed to act?

If you can't bring yourself to say, "You're drunk, and I'm embarrassed," who will?

When you speak up, it's vital that you avoid a nagging, accusatory tone. Keep your statements simple and factual.★ Nagging is just as harmful—and just as tacitly consenting—as silence, because it puts *you* in the wrong and the alcoholic in the right. "I wouldn't *need* to drink if you weren't always hammering at me!" is the kind of defensive response you can expect. Do you see how this puts the focus on *you* and off the real problem?

★For more on this, see *Detachment: Seven Simple Steps.*

Getting You in Your Guilt

. . . .

First we learned to be good little girls and boys. Then
we took on the stereotypes of good wives and husbands
and, later, good parents. We really have been trying so
hard to be good people! And if anyone accuses us of
not living up to our own expectations, we become
terribly guilty and jump to behave as we "should."
Doesn't the alcoholic know this all too well?

So this is what you'll hear from him: "If you really
loved me, you would . . ."; "A good mother would
give me the money for . . ."; "If there's anything I
can't stand it's a nagging wife who . . ."; and the old
standby: "Is it any *wonder* I drink?"

The overriding message in this barrage of guilt-
inducing statements is "Do it *my* way. Lay off my
drinking. (That's sacrosanct.) *You're* the real problem."

But a well-honed sense of guilt doesn't even need
messages from him to trigger it. All those "if only"
thoughts swirl in your head anyway. You know the

kind we mean: "If only I were a better parent, child, lover, cook, housekeeper, worker . . ." To stop that awful, sick feeling of guilt, you'll do just about *anything!*

Now you're really in a jam. The alcoholic has harnessed your guilt to maintain and protect his habit, and you've got yourself believing, "I must be doing something wrong. If I can just figure out how to do it *right,* the bad alcoholic behavior will go away." Do you honestly believe that? This very thought alone can help the alcoholic stay drunk!

Say your hubby comes home smashed and the house is a wreck. You've been to an Al-Anon meeting, a counselor, and a Family Education Program this week (it's only Wednesday), and your hubby's either about to pick a fight and storm out to drink or get you feeling guilty so he can drink peacefully at home.

He starts complaining about the mess and slams a little furniture around for emphasis. "You never do a thing around here," he swears.

Boy, can you feel your guilt and shame coming on! Your mind is already running through the house grabbing the vacuum, the duster, the sponge . . . *but you can stop.* You can tell your guilt to bug off and zero in on the *truth.*

"Yes, you're right, the place *is* a mess. I've been going to several alcoholism programs this week. Right now that's my priority." And you smile gently and walk away.

So your guilt doesn't have to lead you by the nose. Use your brain instead. Listen to the experts, the experienced A.A. and Al-Anon members who know the twists and turns of alcoholic thinking, and your own thinking will begin to straighten out. The best rule may be "Feel guilty if you must, but *don't act on it!*"

Your Sense of Duty

Like guilt, this can backfire on you. You probably have a strong perception of your role and obligations as a parent, spouse, child, friend, employer or employee. You know what these roles mean to you, and when things get out of whack, your sense of duty goes into high gear. Which might be fine if you brought your mind along, but what usually happens goes something like this:

Mother or Father: You gallop off to court to pay your kid's bail (again!), or keep on paying for college even though the return is, at best, a D average!

Wife: You dress in your best to go out for an anniversary dinner with your husband, even though you know that drunkenness will be the main feature of the evening and that there is truly nothing to celebrate.

Husband: You turn down the idea of rehab for your wife or counseling for yourself because a "good" man manages *all* his family's affairs—in private.

Adult child: You eagerly pay your alcoholic mother's rent, thus leaving her with enough extra cash to buy liquor—in short, subsidizing her addiction.

Supervisor: You don't make a negative report about the alcoholic to your boss, because he has been a respected employee for many years and you don't want to "hurt" him or jeopardize his job.

Your kindness and sympathy are misplaced. All these examples are classic enabling behaviors because, in every instance, the alcoholic is given the clear message that *he doesn't have to suffer any consequences for his drinking behavior!* In fact, there *are* no consequences! Every time there's a threat of trouble, the enabler steps in—with the best motives in the world—to smooth things over. With no need to face up to the harsh realities, the alcoholic can sit back, relax . . . and keep on drinking.

Taking Over Responsibilities

. . . .

Often the motivating force behind this type of enabling is simple frustration. Jobs aren't getting done. The alcoholic is so irresponsible that you can expect nothing from him, or so sick that he's barely functioning. And you're beginning to treat him like an incapacitated child, *which fast becomes a self-fulfilling prophecy!* Some examples:

Housewife: You take over paying all the household bills. Terrific! Now the alcoholic doesn't have to deal with or even *see* the financial problems his drinking has created, and he has more time to drink in peace.

Secretary: You notice missed appointments, make calls and excuses, and reschedule meetings at earlier hours, before the martinis have set in. Certainly this will postpone the day when your boss is confronted about his poor job performance; it will also postpone any chance of recovery!

Parents: You allow your 24-year-old unemployed

addict to live at home, rent-free. (But where will he *go?*, you cry!) He has no responsibilities. He's sick, all right, and doesn't have to put an ounce of effort into survival. You've taken that painful, life-sustaining job away from him!

Husband: You come home from work to find your sloshed wife passed out on the sofa. You rush around making dinner for yourself and the kids too, and polish up the kitchen while you're at it. She doesn't have to do a thing!

By all these actions, you say to the alcoholic, "You are unable to do this for yourself because you are incompetent and irresponsible; *I must do it for you.*" The alcoholic's low self-esteem slides ever lower, a negative feeling *that makes alcohol even more necessary and attractive.* And the lack of responsibility allows the drinking to be relatively comfortable and pain-free. (Remember that alcoholics don't confront their addiction until it hurts—a lot!)

Explaining It All Away

Reasonable people look at an alcoholic's irrational behavior and try to make some sense out of it. Ignorant of the nature of addiction, they explain it in their own rational terms. The alcoholic *must* be drinking because of:

• a poor self-image

• a stressful job

• (ten years after) the death of a child

• bad companions

• unemployment or financial problems

• a rotten marriage

• a terrible childhood

Recovering alcoholics know better. Go to an Open Speaker's meeting of Alcoholics Anonymous and you will hear a simple truth: *alcoholics drink because they are alcoholic!* Oh yes, the excessive drinking *may* have been triggered by various problems, but the reverse is more often true: the bad companions, rotten marriage, poor self-image, and financial distress are *results* of drinking, not causes. (Everyone has life traumas, but only alcoholics get drunk for *years* over them!)

Today's repetitive, obsessive, and compulsive drinking stems from *today's addiction!* As A.A. members say, "There are no reasons for drinking, only excuses."

Do you see how the focus is shifting toward the alcoholic and *his* responsibility? We are not refuting alcoholism as a disease—far from it—but we want you to know that one of its salient characteristics is irresponsible behavior. An alcoholic does not get sober until he is *willing to,* and he must recognize his own responsibility in the process. Those who shield him from the consequences are truly enabling: *denying him a chance to recover!*

So you can stop trying to fix the unfixable—the awful past, the stressful present—through misplaced sympathy, psychiatry, or whatever. When the alcoholic comes home late with the excuse that he "stopped off for a few drinks because of a rough day at the office," you can stop enabling him by replying gently, "No, you drank because you're hooked on alcohol and you need help to stop drinking."

Try it. It's a blast of reality. And reality is what will help get the alcoholic *into treatment to stop drinking.*

To Stop Enabling: Three Thoughts

. . . .

First Thought:

Is It Really Helping?

We have assured you that, to stop enabling, all you have to do is *rethink everything you've ever learned to do!* That is strictly the truth, as you've probably discovered. To accomplish this difficult life-and-attitude change, it's helpful to use "mind-stoppers," those little words or signals you use silently within your head to make you pause. Any word that gets you to evaluate your actions is fine: *Whoa! Stop! Hold it! Think!*

Before taking any action, consider the consequences for you as well as for the alcoholic. We're not just talking about crises, but simple daily interactions too. Pause for a moment—use a "mind-stopper" if you like—and ask yourself "Is this thing I want to do (or *not* do) really helpful?" Remember that true help-fulness is the opposite of enabling!

Check it out with the experts. Experienced "Program

People" (A.A. and Al-Anon members) and alcoholism counselors can help you see the distinction between enabling and truly supportive behaviors.

Eventually your new approaches toward the alcoholic will become second nature, but not right away. You may very well feel miserable, guilty, uneasy, and awkward at first when you don't rush to his rescue the way you always did before. This is normal and expected. Just keep talking with the experts!

Second Thought:

Whose Responsibility Is It?

Allowing the alcoholic to experience the full consequences of his drinking is hard. As we've said, it goes against a whole lifetime of training. So "mind-stop" again, and ask yourself (and answer truthfully): "Is it *my* responsibility or *his?*"

For example, he's been convicted of drunk driving and lost his license. Do you drive him to work or leave him to arrange his own transportation? To make this example more difficult (and realistic): If you drive him it's a half-hour trip, and if he takes public transportation it's an hour and a half in the rain and snow and cold. By now, you know full well what *we* think! But saying *no* to the alcoholic for the first time is going to be very rough.

And you will discover soon enough that all his other

"enablers" are against you; suddenly *you're* the bad guy. Friends and relatives will consider you mean. Give them this book to read (it doesn't take long). More important, keep drawing support from Program People. Your stand is a lonely one, and you'll often slip back because the new ways feel so alien.

Sometimes the only way to break enabling behavior is "cold turkey." If you've been successfully manipulated by an alcoholic for a long period, you may have to go so far as not speaking to him or even seeing him for a month or so, in order not to get sucked back in. This period will be like withdrawal—full of guilt, anxiety, and fear—particularly if your decision to stop enabling is still half formed or without conviction.

You will need all the support you can get when the alcoholic starts putting on the pressure. And he will. For a while it's all going to get more tense and uncomfortable. Why? His experience tells him that it's only a matter of time, or finding the right combination, before he breaks you down again!

Remember, you really can't stop enabling all at once. That's expecting too much of yourself. For the first few months, everything will feel worse, and you'll be especially vulnerable. Keep up your Al-Anon meetings and listen to A.A. speakers. In time, it *will* get easier and more natural.

Third Thought:

What Are My Motives?

As you change, expect some confusion in your own mind about your motives. *(All* motives are mixed—and we're so good at rationalizing our actions!) The praise you've gotten for "taking care" of the alcoholic—that is, letting him get away with it—will tempt you back to doing just that. The blame you get when you stop protecting his drinking feels terrible. It's all too comfortable to slide back into the old enabling ways— "for his sake." But your true motive may be the need to return to misery that is at least familiar, or to martyr yourself, or to take the heat off, or to get back to that tried-and-true role of "good person."

Your "de-enabling" program can also get derailed if you become too attached to your role as the only functioning adult in the house. Usually the whole family shifts roles *around* the alcoholic—who, of course, is no longer behaving like a grown-up—and people adjust well to these roles. They don't like their positions challenged. This means that impending sobriety can be a *real threat*—the unknown quantity that's going to force everyone to shift positions once again.

If you keep backsliding into taking over for the alcoholic, or controlling him, you probably *are* threatened by the idea that he might resume his adult role. It's also very tempting to hold on to your righteous anger—but you must set it aside if you're going to become rational about this disease!

You may also find that, as you move away from enabling, something inside you gets a sneaking satisfaction from watching the alcoholic squirm. That's understandable, within limits. But if you get into power-tripping him (playing on vulnerability), there's a danger that you'll lose sight of your original goal: *creating a climate in which sobriety becomes possible.*

Go back to the experts again when you're unsure of your motives. As you struggle to understand what really prompts your actions, their smiles of recognition will help. You know instinctively that they've been there—they're not laughing *at* you, but *with* you.

"Let go," they'll probably tell you; "Let him hurt." And that may be the best advice you will ever get.

Once you slip your fluffy cushion of support out from under him, he'll *notice* the next fall. This is the painful step *you* must take to help him on the road to sobriety. Whether or not he welcomes that new life will depend on *him.*

Symptoms of Alcoholism

. . . .

Does the alcoholic:

1. have a personality change when drinking?
2. suffer memory lapses?
3. have problems at home, at work, or socially because of drinking behavior?
4. cover up or protect drinking?
5. drink more before becoming intoxicated?
6. drink *less* before becoming intoxicated?

Is the alcoholic:

7. making mistakes or having accidents (physical, auto, or mechanical) because of drinking?
8. losing time from duties or responsibilities?
9. angry and defensive about drinking?
10. sneaking or gulping drinks?
11. hiding bottles or cans?

Or is it that:

12. the drinking is bothering *you?*

Suggested Reading

Al-Anon Family Groups, Inc. *Al-Anon's Twelve Steps and Twelve Traditions.* New York: Al-Anon Family Groups, Inc., 1983.

Alcoholics Anonymous World Services, Inc. *Alcoholics Anonymous* ("The Big Book"). 3rd ed. New York: A.A. World Services, Inc., 1976.

Each Day a New Beginning: Daily Meditations for Women. Center City, MN: Hazelden, 1982.

Ray, Veronica. A Moment to Reflect series (collection of four booklets: *Living Our Own Lives, Letting Go, Setting Boundaries, Accepting Ourselves).* Center City, MN: Hazelden, 1989.

Today's Gift: Daily Meditations for Families. Center City, MN: Hazelden, 1985.

All publications listed above are available from

    Hazelden
    Pleasant Valley Road
    P.O. Box 176
    Center City, Minnesota 55012
    1-800-328-9000 (Toll Free U.S., Canada, and the Virgin Islands)
    651-213-4590 (fax)
    hazelden.org

About the Authors

Judith M. Knowlton

Judy has a degree in Psychology from Oberlin College and her Master's in Group Process from Seton Hall University. A recovering alcoholic, she is a Certified Alcoholism Counselor with ten years' experience. Judy has been instrumental in starting several alcoholism programs in northern New Jersey. She is the founder of Action for Sobriety Groups, president of Quotidian, and the mother of three adult children. Her three cats are of varied sizes.

Rebecca D. Chaitin

Becca is a writer and editor, part-time alcoholism counselor, and recovering alcoholic. Born in Virginia, she is a graduate of Hollins College and worked for various New York publishers, including Time-Life Books, before she began freelancing in the early 1970s. She now lives in Montclair, New Jersey, with her three teenagers and three immense cats.

About Hazelden Publishing

As part of the Hazelden Betty Ford Foundation, Hazelden Publishing offers both cutting-edge educational resources and inspirational books. Our print and digital works help guide individuals in treatment and recovery, and their loved ones. Professionals who work to prevent and treat addiction also turn to Hazelden Publishing for evidence-based curricula, digital content solutions, and videos for use in schools, treatment programs, correctional programs, and electronic health records systems. We also offer training for implementation of our curricula.

Through published and digital works, Hazelden Publishing extends the reach of healing and hope to individuals, families, and communities affected by addiction and related issues.

For more information about Hazelden publications,
please call **800-328-9000**
or visit us online at **hazelden.org/bookstore.**

A Gift of Growth

For
. . . .

From
. . . .

Detachment

Detachment

Seven Simple Steps

....

by

JUDITH M. KNOWLTON
and
REBECCA D. CHAITIN

Hazelden
Publishing

Hazelden Publishing
Center City, Minnesota 55012
hazelden.org/bookstore

ISBN: 978-1-59285-746-3

Cover design by Madeline Berglund
Interior design and typesetting by Madeline Berglund

Contents

....

Introduction

It's Going to Take Time!

. . . .

Detachment isn't something you can learn instanta-
neously and permanently. Like sobriety, it will come
gradually, often painfully, and not always smoothly. But
it is not a mystery. It is a manageable, orderly process.

Like many of us, you probably walked into your first
Al-Anon meeting exploding with frustration, anger,
and pain. And when you tried to unload some of it,
chances are one of the old-timers told you, "But you've
got to detach!" So you backed off, confused and hurt,
perhaps believing you had been advised to *ignore* the
alcoholic in your life and stifle your own misery.

That's not detachment! Squashing yourself and your
feelings is a form of denial, and the pressure of your
unresolved anger and pain can only hurt you and
everyone around you.

If you're new and overwhelmed and someone tells
you abruptly to detach, you might respond with,

1

"You're right, I need to do that, but it'll take time—and I don't want to stuff my feelings." That should be a good reminder for you and still keep the lines of communication open.

Detachment is many different things, as you will learn in this book. It is a gradual discovery of the truth about the family disease of alcoholism. It is the process of learning to see things objectively. It is learning to "unhook" yourself emotionally from the alcoholic system. And it is learning at last to act in your own best interest—what's good for *you*—instead of constantly reacting to whatever the alcoholic does.

The result is a new, life-giving attitude. Without it you will stay mired in the destructiveness of the alcoholic system, unable to breathe or take effective action. With it you are on the road to recovery, to emotional health, and the alcoholic's own chances to recover will improve enormously.

Step One

Go Find the Experts

. . . .

You can begin the process of detachment by making a commitment to attend Al-Anon meetings regularly. There you fill find love and support and the experts to help you manage your own life. Remember, they've been there!

Get an Al-Anon sponsor. Look for someone with experience and a positive, no-nonsense attitude, who sees the Twelve Suggested Steps as an *active* program of recovery. Find a person you can talk to on a regular basis, preferably every single day at first.

Plan to attend an open A.A. meeting at least once a month. There you will learn how the alcoholic thinks and what motivates him.★ A.A. members are the experts on how alcoholism feels *from the inside.* You'll discover much about the alcoholic in your life by listening to

---

★Don't take "him" too literally. It can just as easily be "her."

others tell their stories. Even your anger and resentment may dissipate as you gain compassion and objectivity. And in A.A. you'll learn about the joys of recovery and sobriety.

At these meetings, pick up pamphlets and books. Call local and regional alcoholism information numbers—especially the National Council on Alcoholism and Drug Dependence in your area—and ask to be put on mailing lists. Look under "Alcoholism" in the yellow pages of your phone book for other agencies. Collect magazine articles, go to seminars, check the library. Begin by looking for the titles listed in the back of this book. In short, *get informed!* If this were any other chronic, progressive, potentially fatal disease, you would need no urging!

Once you start educating yourself, you will begin to see that you are dealing not with a moral problem, but with a disease that has predictable symptoms. And that's a giant first step toward detachment!

You may want to make an appointment to talk with a professional about the disease. If you do, be certain that the person has been adequately trained in the treatment of alcoholism. Your Al-Anon and A.A. friends will have good recommendations about local experts, and also whom to avoid. Trust their judgment.

At A.A. and Al-Anon meetings, talk to experienced members (you'll soon learn to spot them) rather than

staying with other newcomers who are probably just as confused and uncertain as you. This is called "sticking with the winners," and it's *not* snobbery. It's a vital part of your learning process.

When you meet these people, share experiences, ask questions, and *get their phone numbers*. You are building a support network that will serve you well, and you're *coming out of the isolation that has kept you sick!*

Since alcoholism *is* a treatable disease and not a moral weakness, there are people around you who have a legitimate need to know what you've learned. There will come a time for you to share your discoveries with your children and other close relatives and friends.

Step Two

Take an Inventory

. . . .

This is a twist on Al-Anon's well-known admonition to "*stop* taking his inventory," by which they mean, quite rightly, to stop condemning the alcoholic's behavior while refusing to examine your own.

When we suggest that you *start* taking his inventory, we mean something very different. Start looking at his drinking *objectively,* and pay attention to recurring patterns. No judgments. No blame. Your ultimate aim is a clear-eyed look at the disease process.

For this you'll need a notebook. It will help you maintain your objectivity and spot the patterns. Pay particular attention to the things that seem to trigger drinking episodes. Describe the changes you see in behavior and attitudes. For example, does he pick fights as an excuse to slam out of the house to drink? Does he seesaw between remorse and resentment, or between grandiose expansiveness and utter gloom?

Learn to recognize memory lapses. This alcoholic amnesia may last for moments or even hours or days. The alcoholic appears to behave "normally," but doesn't recall what happened. We call these lapses "blackouts." Does he fish around for clues about what happened the night before, or try to pretend he remembers all about it when he obviously doesn't? Or does he greet the dawn cheerfully after last night's debacle, genuinely puzzled to find you in turmoil?

When you start observing these patterns and writing down the incidents, include the time of day, date, and place. Remember that your goal is to keep a clear and accurate record—what you *see,* not what you *interpret!* You are learning to move away from making judgments and toward making a diagnosis. The list of twelve questions in the back of the book will help you recognize alcoholic behavior patterns, and at some point you will accept them as recurring symptoms of a chronic and progressive disease.

Step Three

Report Your Diagnosis

. . . .

Your next step is to find a receptive, knowledgeable listener—a trusted friend in A.A. or Al-Anon, your sponsor, or a counselor with alcoholism training—and describe what you have seen. (This should be done in private. You will need to ventilate some feelings, and an Al-Anon meeting is *not* the place for it!)

Choose your listener with care. When you report your observations for the first time, some of those rotten feelings are bound to pour out of you. Your listener must be able to function as a calm, nonjudgmental sounding board; anyone who sees alcoholism as a moral issue obviously won't do. Once you've started "dumping the garbage," you will begin to gain objectivity about your situation, and talking about it rationally will become a lot easier.

As your objectivity—and emotional detachment, which may be the same thing—increases, you'll find

your own residual denial beginning to crumble. But this happens slowly. You may catch yourself thinking, "Maybe it really *is* my fault, like he's always saying; maybe if I were different, he wouldn't have to drink . . ." Baloney! Once you start observing an alcoholic with a clear eye, you'll see that he really *does* have a disease— an inexorable and progressive disease that follows certain patterns *no matter what you do!*

You are not the cause, and you no longer have to bear the burden of tying yourself (and everyone around you) in knots in order to "make" him stop drinking.

Step Four

Focus on Yourself

. . . .

You probably realize by now that the alcoholic's illness is not your fault, but you may not be fully aware of the damage done to you. Indeed, as you will hear at meetings, *you are sick too.* And who wouldn't be? It is normal to behave abnormally in an abnormal situation! Look at it another way: you've spent all that emotional energy trying to make things right, and *it has not worked!* Your life has been so focused on him and his disease, you probably don't even know what your own needs are, much less what you *want* for yourself.

You *must* focus on yourself to survive. Begin by getting into the Al-Anon program in depth. And don't hide your involvement in Al-Anon by attending meetings only when the alcoholic is out of the house! No speeches, but he needs to know that you are working on *your* recovery. Keep in touch with your sponsor, which means calling early and often, preferably *before*

a crisis. Don't wait until after disaster strikes.

It is time to work Al-Anon's Twelve Steps in earnest, with emphasis on Steps Four and Five.★ Both steps will chip away at your denial and allow you to focus on yourself. Remember to take the old-timers' suggestion to heart: don't acknowledge a defect in yourself until you can balance it with an asset. Putting yourself down isn't honest or true. Labeling yourself as worthless is a way of staying irresponsible!

As you work the Steps and start "unhooking" from the alcoholism, keep asking yourself, "What do *I* want?" For example, you might practice statements like "I want to live in a sober environment"; "I want to stop accepting unacceptable behavior"; "I want to feel good about myself." (If your statement begins with, "I want *him* to . . . ," stop right there. You're on the wrong track!)

By focusing on *your* wants and needs, and what you can *do* for yourself, you avoid a lot of pitfalls, such as trying to follow the dictates of a society that doesn't understand alcoholism, giving in to martyrdom (a real temptation, because you'll be praised for it by those who don't know better!), or trying to force the alcoholic to straighten out. All of these are surely exercises in futility.

★The Twelve Steps are in the back of this book.

When you focus on yourself in a positive, growth-oriented way, you get back all the emotional energy you've been investing so uselessly in the alcoholic. And heaven knows, you need it!

Step Five

Discover Your Bottom Line

. . . .

This is a tough step, and it may take you several months. Don't rush it. Discovering your bottom line means making an honest, realistic determination of *what you will no longer put up with and what you will do about it*. You'll need to examine alternatives very carefully, and go over them at length with an experienced counselor or Al-Anon member. For anyone who has spent years reacting to the overwhelming destructiveness of alcoholism—dreading the worst, shouldering the blame, swallowing the pain, being battered or verbally abused—this is both difficult and crucial.

Think out possible bottom lines carefully, and *don't use them to manipulate the alcoholic!* They have to be designed for *you,* in your own best interest. Above all, *don't threaten anything you're not prepared to carry through!*

Bottom lines, incidentally, are not just the big moves

for dealing with the alcoholism "once and for all." They come in all sorts of everyday sizes too. You can make some positive, goal-setting bottom lines for yourself, such as I will attend *no fewer* than three Al-Anon meetings each week; I will talk to someone in the program *daily;* I will remember to do something good for myself *every day.*

When you examine bottom lines in relation to the alcoholic, start by considering a small one you know you can stick to rather than one you might have to back away from later. Suppose, for example, that you've been filling your head with panic and projections about what he's up to, or what will become of him, or what will become of *you,* or what the neighbors will think! *This is useless, gut-churning, obsessive thinking,* and it leaves you drained and helpless. So, next time you catch yourself wallowing in the woe, you might declare a bottom line that says, "I will *not* indulge myself in this; I will call my sponsor right now" (or make plans with a friend, or simply leave the house). As you will discover, once you refocus your attention on your own needs and wants, the obsessive thinking begins to fade away.

At some point down the line, you may well conclude that you can no longer accept the drinking at all. The more detached you have become, the more clearly you will see what your options are.

Step Six

Make a Decision

....

This step is a natural outgrowth of the previous one. It's almost impossible to separate them, because by now you have begun to *act for yourself.* You are gradually detaching from the alcoholic system and its twisted, blame-oriented thinking, and you have examined many bottom lines. You are already making small, satisfying decisions. You may have found your confidence increasing as you put your bottom lines into practice. It has become much easier to deliberate, to decide, to do! You are at last ready to declare: *beyond this I will not go, period!*

Again, make your choices carefully. No one else, no matter how experienced or empathetic, can choose your bottom line (or lines) for you. You're the one who must live with your decision. And realize, too, that if you make a mistake—if you choose a bottom line that turns out not to work for you—*you can change it!*

None of us has totally pure motives, but it's crucial that you make decisions based on what's best for you. If you still secretly hope that you can somehow *maneuver* the alcoholic into sobriety, you're kidding yourself. Your decision must be *for you,* not for him—*about you,* not about him.★

★Ask an alcoholism counselor about intervention, a professionally directed program that can help an alcoholic into treatment.

Step Seven

Take Charge of Your Life

. . . .

As you continue to work the previous six steps, appropriate decisions and actions will come as a logical and natural outgrowth of what you are learning. We are quick to acknowledge that this is a "selfish program," but by that we mean a program of *enlightened self-interest*. Rather than asking in a given situation, "How can I *fix* that?" you are, we hope, beginning to ask yourself, *"How do I choose to respond?"*

Strangely—and wonderfully—as you become more focused on your own needs and wants, you become willing to break the old destructive patterns that left you feeling bruised, worthless, and hopelessly stuck. The more you take charge of your life, the more your self-esteem rises and the more willing you become to take responsible action *and to accept the consequences of your decisions.* You begin to know when to act and, just as important, when *not* to act; when to be silent, when to speak up; when to confront and when to walk away.

And you need not force detachment; you'll know it when it comes. *It feels different!* Somehow that rigid self-control disappears and in its place there is a calm, secure sense of self—a positive "I" feeling.

Be proud of your growth, but don't expect to become perfect. Oh yes, you *will* get caught in the alcoholic's web now and again. *You're human.* Be kind to yourself when it happens. You can say to yourself, with a little humor, "Oops, suckered again!" and then move on.

When the alcoholic behaves self-destructively (which may be most of the time), you no longer believe his rationalizations and excuses, because you see his illness for what it is. And yet somehow you no longer feel helplessly enmeshed in it. That's the difference. One day you'll find yourself saying something like "I don't know how it happened, but he came home stinking drunk and I simply *wasn't afraid*. I didn't even want to tell him off. I told him I'd be home at eleven, put on my coat, and left for my regular Al-Anon meeting."

In the broadest sense, these seven steps to detachment have nothing whatever to do with alcoholism. They are equally effective in helping you assess *all* your relationships. Indeed, once you've learned the process of detachment, you may find yourself dealing with *everyone* in a more honest, realistic, and productive way.

No one promises that you're going to walk off into some Hollywood sunset. Instead, these steps direct

your path toward something far more enduring and satisfying. Do you recognize it now? It is the *real* miracle of personal growth. You are at last discovering *you*.

Al-Anon's Twelve Steps

· ·

—— One ——

We admitted we were powerless over alcohol—that our lives had become unmanageable.

—— Two ——

Came to believe that a Power greater than ourselves could restore us to sanity.

—— Three ——

Made a decision to turn our will and our lives over to the care of God *as we understood Him.*

—— Four ——

Made a searching and fearless moral inventory of ourselves.

—— Five ——

Admitted to God, to ourselves, and to another human being the exact nature of our wrongs.

—— Six ——

Were entirely ready to have God remove all these defects of character.

—— Seven ——

Humbly asked Him to remove our shortcomings.

—— Eight ——

Made a list of all persons we had harmed, and became willing to make amends to them all.

—— Nine ——

Made direct amends to such people wherever possible, except when to do so would injure them or others.

—— Ten ——

Continued to take personal inventory and when we were wrong promptly admitted it.

—— Eleven ——

Sought through prayer and meditation to improve our conscious contact with God *as we understood Him,* praying only for knowledge of His will for us and the power to carry that out.

—— Twelve ——

Having had a spiritual awakening as a result of these steps, we tried to carry this message to others, and to practice these principles in all our affairs.

Questions for an Inventory

Does the alcoholic:

1. have a personality change when drinking?
2. suffer memory lapses?
3. have problems at home, at work, or socially because of drinking behavior?
4. cover up or protect drinking?
5. drink more before becoming intoxicated?
6. drink *less* before becoming intoxicated?

Is the alcoholic:

7. making mistakes or having accidents (physical, auto, or mechanical) because of drinking?
8. losing time from duties or responsibilities?
9. angry and defensive about drinking?
10. sneaking or gulping drinks?
11. hiding bottles or cans?

Or is it that:

12. the drinking is bothering *you?*

Suggested Reading

Al-Anon Family Groups, Inc. *Al-Anon's Twelve Steps and Twelve Traditions.* New York: Al-Anon Family Groups, Inc., 1983.

Alcoholics Anonymous World Services, Inc. *Alcoholics Anonymous* ("The Big Book"). 3rd ed. New York: A.A. World Services, Inc., 1976.

Each Day a New Beginning: Daily Meditations for Women. Center City, MN: Hazelden, 1982.

Ray, Veronica. A Moment to Reflect series (collection of four booklets: *Living Our Own Lives, Letting Go, Setting Boundaries, Accepting Ourselves).* Center City, MN: Hazelden, 1989.

Today's Gift: Daily Meditations for Families. Center City, MN: Hazelden, 1985.

All publications listed above are available from
> Hazelden
> Pleasant Valley Road
> P.O. Box 176
> Center City, Minnesota 55012
> 1-800-328-9000 (Toll Free U.S., Canada, and the Virgin Islands)
> 651-213-4590 (fax)
> hazelden.org

About the Authors

. . . .

Judith M. Knowlton

Judy has a degree in Psychology from Oberlin College
and her Master's in Group Process from Seton Hall
University. A recovering alcoholic, she is a Certified
Alcoholism Counselor with ten years' experience.
Judy has been instrumental in starting several alco-
holism programs in northern New Jersey. She is the
founder of Action for Sobriety Groups, president of
Quotidian, and the mother of three adult children.
Her three cats are of varied sizes.

Rebecca D. Chaitin

Becca is a writer and editor, part-time alcoholism
counselor, and recovering alcoholic. Born in Virginia,
she is a graduate of Hollins College and worked for
various New York publishers, including Time-Life
Books, before she began freelancing in the early 1970s.
She now lives in Montclair, New Jersey, with her three
teenagers and three immense cats.

About Hazelden Publishing

As part of the Hazelden Betty Ford Foundation, Hazelden Publishing offers both cutting-edge educational resources and inspirational books. Our print and digital works help guide individuals in treatment and recovery, and their loved ones. Professionals who work to prevent and treat addiction also turn to Hazelden Publishing for evidence-based curricula, digital content solutions, and videos for use in schools, treatment programs, correctional programs, and electronic health records systems. We also offer training for implementation of our curricula.

Through published and digital works, Hazelden Publishing extends the reach of healing and hope to individuals, families, and communities affected by addiction and related issues.

For more information about Hazelden publications,
please call **800-328-9000**
or visit us online at **hazelden.org/bookstore.**